The Ism Book
A Field Guide to
Philosophy

Peter Saint-Andre

For further information about the book,
including the online version, visit
http://ismbook.com/

For other books by the author, visit
https://stpeter.im/

Published by the Monadnock Valley Press,
Parker, Colorado
http://www.monadnock.net/

ISBN: 0615879616

ISBN-13: 978-0615879611

The Ism Book

Absolutism

[From Latin absolutum: detached, independent, completed.]

Religion: Within some forms of Christianity (especially Calvinism), the doctrine that one's salvation is predestined and determined solely by the will of God, uninfluenced by reasons such as one's deeds or intentions; more commonly called the doctrine of predestination.

Politics: The doctrine that a sovereign or government ought to possess absolute power over individuals and society; an older and less common term for totalitarianism.

Abstractionism

[From Latin abstractus: drawn away or out from, derived, removed, separated.]

Metaphysics: The doctrine that ideas or abstractions actually exist; see idealism and Platonism.

Epistemology: The view that knowledge is gained only through abstraction from particulars; more commonly called conceptualism.

Aesthetics: The doctrine that artistic abstraction is more valuable or important than representation, especially in the visual arts; see modernism and expressionism.

Accidentalism

[From Latin accidere: to fall or happen.]

Metaphysics: The idea, similar to indeterminism, that some events simply happen; this idea is one aspect of some defenses of freedom of the will (see libertarianism).

Aestheticism

[From Greek aisthetikos: pertaining to perception; extended to refer to perception of the beautiful by Alexander Baumgarten.]

Ethics: The idea that the highest values are aesthetic rather than ethical or religious. This idea is often associated with nineteenth-century romanticism in general, and personally with Friedrich Schiller (author of *The Aesthetic Education of Man*) and Friedrich Nietzsche, both of whom sometimes advocated the goal of making one's life a work of art.

Agnosticism

[From Greek agnostos: unknowing, unknown, unknowable.]

Epistemology: The idea that one cannot know whether or not gods exist. Agnosticism adopts a "wait-and-see" attitude toward the existence of gods (similar in this regard to skepticism) and therefore is different from atheism, which positively asserts that gods do not exist.

Altruism

[Coined by Auguste Comte from French autrui, descended from Latin alter: other.]

Ethics: Regard for the welfare of other people (as opposed to one's own welfare) as the highest principle of action. While one could, in theory, describe altruism as a form of eudaimonism since since it seeks to maximize happiness, eudaimonism is always taken to be a kind of individualism or egoism (and therefore in opposition to altruism). Strictly speaking, Kantianism and other forms of deontologism are not variants of altruism since they emphasize conformance with duty or moral law rather than concern for other people. In general, altruism emphasizes either the intent to benefit others (see intentionalism) or the practical result that one's actions do indeed benefit others (see consequentialism). Often altruistic doctrines are universalized, as in utilitarianism (which holds that the highest ethical principle is "the greatest good for the greatest number"). The popular meaning of altruism is loosely connected to the philosophical meaning, and usually refers to an attitude of benevolence toward other people.

Anarchism

[From Greek anarchos: lacking a leader.]

Politics: Anarchism is inspired by the moral-political ideal of a society untouched by relations of power and domination among human beings. This ideal has most often expressed itself in a doctrine advocating the total absence of government as the only firm basis for individual liberty and societal progress – a doctrine that some argue animates even Marxism (since Marx believed that eventually the state would wither away). Anarchism differs from political libertarianism in upholding a lack of government rather than limited government. There are several variants of anarchism, usually categorized by whether the variant is collectivistic (e.g., anarcho-syndicalism) or individualistic (e.g., anarcho-capitalism) in orientation. In popular usage, the term is often colored by the sometimes-violent anarchist political movement that was especially active in the years around 1900.

Animism

[From Latin anima: the breath or soul of a living being.]

Religion: The idea that living spirits inhabit every existing thing (similar to but distinct from pantheism).

Anthropocentrism

[From Greek anthropos: human being, and from Latin centrum: middle point.]

Ethics: The doctrine that humanity is the central fact of existence and that all ethical matters are to be gauged by how they affect human interests.

Antinomianism

[From Greek anti against, and from Greek nomos: law.]

Ethics: The doctrine that moral laws are not obligatory or do not apply those who have been graced with the favor of god.

Apriorism

[From Latin a priori: that which comes before.]

Epistemology: The view (opposed to empiricism) that some or all knowledge can be gained without reference to experience.

Aristotelianism

[From the name of the Greek philosopher Aristotle (384-322 BCE).]

System: Aristotle was the first philosopher to create a more-or-less complete system of thought. In particular, he originated or gave renewed force to individualism, eudaimonism, optimism, realism, humanism, naturalism, and even to a certain extent political liberalism (in that he defended the importance of voluntary institutions and the rule of law). Unfortunately, because of the history of Aristotle's writings in the West (they disappeared for centuries only to be rediscovered again around 1200 CE at the height of the logicism of the Middle Ages), Aristotle often is blamed for the mistakes and views of his interpreters. Thus the popular conception of Aristotelianism is sometimes closer to neo-Platonism or especially scholasticism than anything Aristotle argued for in his writings. In addition to his work in philosophy, Aristotle founded the science of logic and performed significant research in biology, political science, rhetoric, literary theory, and many other disciplines.

Asceticism

[From Greek asketes: a hermit or monk; derived from askesis: practice, training, mode of life.]

Ethics: Originally, an ascetic was one who practiced the mode of life of a hermit or monk, characterized by solitude, meditation, prayer, toil, fasting, and celibacy. Implicit in this lifestyle of self-discipline and self-denial is the idea that the pleasures of this world should be renounced in favor of a 'higher' purpose such as intellectual discipline or mystical insight. Often asceticism is connected to either spiritualism or rationalism. For the opposite view, see sensualism.

Ascriptivism

[From English ascribe: to attribute something to someone.]

Metaphysics: The view that human beings are to be held responsible for their actions even if determinism is true.

Associationalism

[From Latin adsociare: to join or combine together.]

Epistemology: A theory of knowledge holding that all concepts are formed through the customary or even arbitrary connection of an image or mental idea with an object (based on similarity, closeness in space or time, etc.). The principle of association was first expressed by John Locke (1632-1704) and extended by David Hume (1711-1776). In various forms, associationalism dominated Anglo-American thinking about epistemology for hundreds of years: it was formalized into a thoroughgoing theory of knowledge in the 19th century (in tandem with sensationalism), and replacing philosophical "concepts" with psychological "stimulus-response interactions" yielded behaviorism in the 20th century.

Atheism

[A privative term derived from Greek theos: god.]

Metaphysics: Atheism is an active disbelief in the existence of gods, deities, and supernatural powers; in this respect it is similar to secularism and opposed to any variety of theism. Atheism is to be contrasted with agnosticism, which takes a skeptical attitude toward the existence of gods but does not proclaim disbelief. Popularly, atheism is often taken to imply a lack of any ideals or values whatsoever (nearly equivalent to immoralism), but this connotation rests on an assumption that religion is the only foundation for values (thus ignoring the possibility of naturalism).

Atomism

[From Greek atomos: indivisible.]

Metaphysics: Any metaphysical or cosmological idea that reality is fundamentally made up only of extremely small, indivisible particles. This view was widespread among ancient Greek philosophers such as Democritus (460?-362? BCE) and Epicurus, and was revived in the 17th century by philosophers such as Pierre Gassendi and scientists such as Robert Boyle, the founder of modern chemistry.

Authoritarianism

[From French autorite: power or right to enforce obedience.]

Politics: The idea that a leader or government possesses moral or legal supremacy and the right to command others without their consent. Although authoritarianism is sometimes considered to involve a less egregious violation of human rights than totalitarianism, it is still actively opposed to any form of democratic liberalism or libertarianism.

Automatism

[From Greek automatismos: that which happens on its own.]

Metaphysics: The doctrine that the actions of animals are mechanistically determined. In particular, this doctrine is one constituent of Cartesianism, since Descartes (1596-1650) advocated a strict determinism or mechanism in biology. Although automatism has little basis in biological fact, its core beliefs have persisted into recent times under different names (e.g., see behaviorism).

Behaviorism

[From English behavior: the manner in which a person, animal, or thing acts, either characteristically or in particular circumstances.]

Psychology: The doctrine that only a person's or animal's externally observed ways of acting provide legitimate data for the study of psychology. As originally formulated by John D. Watson in 1913, behaviorism was a methodological principle defined in order to pursue scientific objectivity in psychology. However, the behaviorist movement (pushed forward by prominent psychologists such as B.F. Skinner and influenced by scientific operationalism) soon came to dismiss any internal states, mental phenomena, or higher-order emergent properties of living beings. The result was a kind of reductionism, materialism, or even automatism applied to animal and human activity, which in its more radical forms did not even seek to reduce consciousness to stimulus-response interactions, but simply ignored mental phenomena altogether. From the 1960s onwards, behaviorism was supplanted by psychological cognivitism and more recently by evolutionary psychology.

Buddhism

[From Sanskrit budh: to awaken or to know.]

Religion: In ancient India, a buddha was a person who had achieved deep or even divine enlightenment. The historical Buddha of Buddhist thought was Gautama Siddhartha (c. 563-483 BCE), who lived a life of detachment from worldly affairs, distrust of perceptual appearance and social conventions, inner-directed reflection and meditation, and suppression of pain, sorrow, and desire. Traditionally, Buddhism has stressed self-denial (similar to Stoicism but sometimes bordering on asceticism), the unity of all things (see holism), and a kind of spiritualized individualism. Although Buddhists consider Gautama to be divine, Buddhism is not a form of theism in the Western sense. Through the centuries, several major schools of Buddhist thought emerged (most prominently Mahayana and Theravada) and Buddhist ideas were combined with traditional Chinese beliefs like Taoism, resulting in Ch'an (or Zen) Buddhism. In fact, Buddhism is quite similar to Taoism in many ways, although Buddhism is closer to transcendentalism since it puts a greater value on ultimate detachment and eternal enlightenment, a state known as nirvana.

Capitalism

[Back-formed from English capitalist, one who possesses capital; from English capital: the primary or principal wealth of an individual or corporation, mainly as used for investment in production; derived from Latin capitalis: relating to the head, chief, foremost.]

Politics: Originally came capital (first use: 1611), then came men of capital or capitalists (first use: 1792), then came capitalism (first use: 1854). In essence, the word capitalism describes a society that favors or encourages the formation and investment of wealth in production. In this sense, capitalism is often synonymous with the economic relations that emerge naturally in the absence of political control. Although this kind of free-market or laissez-faire capitalism is opposed by political philosophies such as socialism and communism and allied with political philosophies such as classical liberalism and libertarianism, numerous economists and social theorists insist that market phenomena emerge organically from human trading and therefore that capitalism is not an "ism" in the ideological sense. However, it is probably worthwhile to distinguish between capitalism and markets, since pure market relations would not necessarily favor the kind of corporate powers that are often artificially protected by contemporary legal systems and political ideologies. Although "natural" markets may favor the creation of capital, not everything that favors the creation of capital is natural or non-ideological.

Cartesianism

[From the name of the French philosopher Rene Descartes (1596-1650).]

Metaphysics: Descartes is often considered the founder of modern philosophy (although his ideas owed much to medieval thinkers such as Avicenna). The signature ideas of Cartesianism are dualism, rationalism, and the mind-body dichotomy (i.e., a combination of idealism in the spiritual realm and of mechanism in the physical realm).

Christianity

[From Greek christos: anointed.]

Religion: Christianity is the name given to the religion and (later) theology that arose among those who considered Jesus of Nazareth (c. 3 BCE - 26 CE) to be the "Lord's Anointed" (messiah) of ancient Jewish prophecy. Its signature ideas include the redemptive power of belief in Jesus as the Christ, original sin caused by human knowledge of good and evil, the intrinsic worth of all individuals, and altruistic love (agape). In its early centuries, Christianity experienced its share of doctrinal disputes but started out mainly as a religious community with its own set of practices and beliefs but not as an explicitly philosophical theology. The development of early Christian theology owes much to the neo-Platonism of Augustine (354-430), including powerful strains of transcendentalism, metaphysical dualism, and a kind of tempered mysticism. In the late Middle Ages, Thomas Aquinas (1225?-1274 CE) turned Christian theology more towards Aristotelianism; however, the secularism, rationalism, and holism of the Aristotelian world-view are fundamentally at odds with Christianity (although attempts to combine the two persist until today and are often called neo-Aristotelianism).

Classicism

[From Latin classicus: of the highest class, of the first order.]

Aesthetics: In common usage, classicism describes an emphasis or over-emphasis on past (especially Greek and Latin) practice, examples, and rules, mainly in the making of art. In aesthetics, classicism is usually contrasted historically and philosophically with romanticism.

Cognitivism

[From Latin cognito: knowledge.]

Metaphysics: The view that knowledge is a major, even primary, determinant of human behavior; developed in reaction to behaviorism as a result of the "cognitive revolution" in psychology.

Ethics: Another word for intellectualism.

Coherentism

[From Latin coherere: to stick together.]

Epistemology: The view that a statement is true because of its relationship to or coherence with other statements in a consistent network or system of statements.

Collectivism

[From Latin colligere: to gather together.]

Politics: A doctrine in political philosophy (and sometimes ethics) holding that the individual's actions should benefit not the individual but some kind of collective organization (such as a tribe, community, profession, or state). Collectivism in political theory depends on altruism in ethics. There are many forms of collectivism in political reality, such as tribalism, communism, socialism, fascism, certain forms of trade unionism, authoritarianism, totalitarianism, and communalism. The term is most often associated with totalitarian governments of the twentieth century, but is uncommon in everyday language.

Communalism

[From French and Latin communal: of a commune or community.]

Politics: Communalism is a kind of small-scale utopianism or voluntary collectivism. Political communalists sometimes posit that local communities should have virtual autonomy within the context of a larger state or society (similar to Robert Nozick's concept of meta-utopia). Nonpolitical communalists simply build intentional communities.

Communism

[From Latin communis: shared by all.]

Politics: The political theory that an individual's actions should benefit the community or the state rather than the individual. It is the most radical kind of political collectivism, and depends on an equally radical altruism in ethics. In practice, communism has always been a form of totalitarianism. When referring to actual political systems, communism is sometimes called Marxism-Leninism because of communism's link with the revolutionary doctrines of Marxism and with countries inspired by the example of Lenin's revolution in Russia (and Mao's revolution in China). Communism is sometimes also called international socialism in contrast to the national socialism of fascism.

Communitarianism

[From Latin communitas: community or fellowship.]

Politics: In the nineteenth century, the word "communitarian" referred to members of voluntary communities formed to put socialist or communist ideas into practice (close to the more recent usage of the term communalism). In the 1990s, a movement of intellectuals resuscitated the term to mount a philosophical and political challenge to the seeming triumph of market liberalism, stressing the importance of fellowship and community over economic relations and market interactions.

Compatibilism

[From Latin compatibilis: sympathetic or mutually tolerant.]

Metaphysics: The view that a full physical description of the brain would be compatible with the subjective experience of volition; contrast with incompatibilism, libertarianism, and determinism.

Conceptualism

[From Latin conceptum: something conceived, an idea.]

Epistemology: The view that conceptual knowledge consists of non-arbitrary abstractions from perceptual knowledge, but that concepts do not have an independent existence. Conceptualism thus opposes both nominalism and realism. Although the main conceptualist in philosophical history was Peter Abailard (1079-1142), Aristotelianism is also sometimes considered to be a form of conceptualism.

Concretism

[From English concrete: a material thing or actual reality as opposed to an abstract quality, state, or activity; derived from Latin concretus: grown together.]

Metaphysics: The view that, fundamentally, the only existents are concrete entities or material things (i.e., that there are no actual universals or non-material existents); similar to materialism and particularism.

Confucianism

[From the name of the Chinese sage K'ung Fu Tzu (550-480 BCE).]

Ethics: Confucianism is the main stream of Chinese philosophy, just as Western philosophy is mostly in the Socratic tradition. Although the views of Confucius have been interpreted in various ways throughout history, no one denies that they are a powerful variety of humanism. Confucius held that the most important, indeed sacred, aspect of life is one's dealings with other people, and he put great emphasis on virtues such as honesty, justice, and integrity. Although the Confucian tradition has been fairly conservative (similar in this respect to Aristotelianism), often when people talk about Confucianism they are referring not so much to the actual views of Confucius as to the way his writings were used by later interpreters to justify reactionary political practices such as a large bureaucracy and the stratification of society.

Consequentialism

[From English consequential: following something else, especially as an effect or result; derived from Latin consequi: to follow closely.]

Ethics: The view that ethical decisions are best or properly be made on the basis of the expected outcome or consequences of the action. Both pragmatism and utilitarianism are forms of consequentialism. Because consequentialism tends to focus on the impact of an action on persons other than the actor, in general it is a variety of altruism rather than egoism.

Conservatism

[From Latin conservare: to keep or preserve.]

Method: Any approach to philosophy or a related discipline that seeks to preserve established practices or that resists change (e.g., classicism in aesthetics).

Politics: A political approach or movement that preserves existing institutions or that opposes changes to the established order of society (in opposition to liberalism or progressivism).

Constructivism

[From English construct: to make by fitting together constituent parts, or to form in the mind; derived from Latin construere: to pile up, to build.]

Epistemology: A radical kind of subjectivism positing that reality does not exist outside of human conceptions, and that human beings form or construct reality through the activity of their minds.

Contextualism

[From Latin contextus: connected or weaved together.]

Metaphysics: The view that all entities are connected together; another word for holism.

Epistemology: The view that an entity cannot be known without understanding the full context of its connections to other entities.

Ethics: The view that ethical value is not absolute but dependent on a specific personal, historical, or societal context.

Aesthetics: The view that a work of art can be interpreted only in the light of its historical context.

Conventionalism

[From English conventional: arbitrarily or artificially determined, in accordance with accepted standards of truth, conduct, or taste; derived from Latin conventionem: meeting or assembly.]

Epistemology: A form of social subjectivism or relativism holding that truth, good, and beauty are merely a matter of arbitrary or artificial social convention and are not objective or naturalistic in any way.

Creationism

[From Latin creare: to make or produce.]

Metaphysics: The doctrine (opposed to eternalism) that the universe was created by a god (usually the Christian god) out of nothingness.

Religion: The doctrine (opposed to Darwinism) that living things, and especially human beings, were created by a god and did not evolve from earlier life forms.

Cynicism

[From Greek kunikos: dog-like, churlish.]

Ethics: The ancient Greek school of Cynic philosophers, founded by Antisthenes (a student of Socrates), held that pure virtue is the only good and cultivated an asceticism more rigorous than that of Epicureanism or Stoicism. Because of their disdain for worldly concerns, the Cynics were critical of conventional morality and the rest of society, almost to the point of misanthropy.

Darwinism

[From the name of the English biologist Charles Darwin (1809-1882).]

Biology: The theory (strictly speaking biological rather than philosophical) that all living things have descended from earlier common ancestors through processes of biological evolution such as natural selection; opposed by creationism.

Deconstructionism

[A term coined by the French critic Jacques Derrida (1930-2004).]

Aesthetics: A late twentieth-century theory of literature that concentrates on finding "ruptures" or inconsistencies in a text, thus enabling the critic to break it down or "deconstruct" it. Such deconstruction consists of asserting a personally or communally relative interpretation (usually focused on power relations or class conflict in society) without claiming that any text or interpretation has objective truth or meaning. Deconstructionism is a specific kind of postmodernism, and leans heavily toward subjectivism or even nihilism.

Deism

[From Latin deus: god.]

Religion: The idea, formulated during the Enlightenment of the 1600s and 1700s, that God created the universe but then left it alone to operate on its own principles – principles that human reason and scientific inquiry can discover. According to deism, God is not involved in the day-to-day workings of the universe and there are no miracles. Historically, deism was a kind of way station between the theism of the Middle Ages and the agnosticism or outright atheism of modern times.

Deontologism

[From Greek deontos: that which is binding, right, proper.]

Ethics: Emphasis on universal imperatives such moral laws, duties, obligations, prohibitions, or imperatives (thus sometimes also called imperativism). Kantianism is the prime example of a deontological theory. Deontologism is usually contrasted with teleologism (an emphasis on goals) and consequentialism (an emphasis on results), but sometimes is also contrasted with egoism and eudaimonism (an emphasis on personal happiness or fulfillment as opposed to conformance with moral imperatives). In practice, deontologism is often closely allied with ethical intuitionism.

Descriptivism

[From English descriptive: represented in words by reference to actual qualities; derived from Latin describere: to copy off or transcribe.]

Ethics: The view that ethics merely represents or describes how human beings act in real life and that ethics cannot prescribe normative human values. English philosopher David Hume (1711-1776) and Italian political theorist Niccolo Machiavelli (1469-1527) are often characterized as descriptivists. The opposing view is prescriptivism.

Determinism

[From English determine: to ordain or fix beforehand; derived from Latin determinare: to limit or bound.]

Metaphysics: The belief that all physical events and human actions are fixed or ordained by external forces before they happen. Determinists deny the existence of chosen human activity ("free will"), and the more consistent determinists deny that people bear any responsibility for their actions. Determinists are usually adherents of materialism, although some social or economic determinists are more influenced by Marxism than by the advance of physics, chemistry, and biology. In popular usage, determinism has connotations of fatalism. In more technical discussions, determinism is sometimes called necessitarianism, in opposition to metaphysical libertarianism.

Dialectical Materialism

[From Greek dialektikos: relating to dialogue or discussion, and Latin materia: physical stuff.]

Politics: A form of historical determinism espoused by Marxism. The dialetical aspect derives from Hegelianism, which holds that history proceeds in something like the stages of a conversation, with each stage overcoming the previous stages and therefore coming closer to finally attained unity or truth. The materialist aspect replaced Hegel's emphasis on spiritual improvement and the collective unconscious with a focus on economic classes and the economic-technological basis for social relations. Thus dialectical materialism posits that history progresses in stages that are based solely on ownership of the means of production: i.e., feudalism replaced aristocracy, capitalism replaced feudalism, and true socialism or communism will replace capitalism – all according to inexorable, immutable laws.

Dogmatism

[From Greek dogma: belief, opinion, tenet, doctrine, decree.]

Method: A style of philosophy that emphasizes rigid adherence to doctrine over rational and enlightened inquiry. The opposite approach is probably best characterized as rationalism (in the sense of devotion to clear reasoning and independent thinking) or eclecticism.

Dualism

[From Latin dualis: containing two.]

Metaphysics: A doctrine in metaphysics or cosmology positing that there are only two fundamental things, substances, or aspects of reality in the universe at large or in human psychology. The first influential dualist theory in Western philosophy was Platonism, since Plato claimed that there are two different realities: the physical world of appearances and the higher world of intelligible forms, ideas, or essences, with a similar separation in the human person between mind and body. These ideas were assimilated by Stoicism and, later, by Christianity. While dualism was influential throughout the Christian era, it received renewed impetus from Descartes, who held that reality is made up exclusively of spirit and matter, and that these two substances can never meet or interact -- except in the human soul (which gives rise to the modern mind-body dichotomy). Aristotelianism, by contrast, generally holds that mind and body are not two distinct substances but two aspects of a complete human person (cf. holism). Even though dualism is a kind of metaphysical pluralism and is opposed by monism, practically speaking dualists often emphasize the 'higher', more spiritual reality, so that they are often construed as adherents of idealism or transcendentalism.

Dynamism

[From Greek dynamis: power, force, energy.]

Metaphysics: The idea that the universe fundamentally consists of changeable forces or energies rather than stable entities. Dynamism is often augmented by the notion that much of the stability we perceive is illusory and that everything is constantly changing or in flux (sometimes called a Heraclitean view of the universe, after the ancient Greek philosopher Heraclitus). The best-known dynamists of recent times were Alfred North Whitehead and Henri Bergson (called "process philosophers" because they focused on processes rather than entities).

Eclecticism

[From Greek eklektikos: selective.]

Method: An approach to philosophy that does not respect the boundaries of existing schools or systems, but instead selects ideas from each. The term is often applied in a negative way, implying a lack of either philosophical consistency or systematic thinking.

Egalitarianism

[From French egalite: equality.]

Politics: The view that equality is the most important societal (and even ethical) value. Egalitarians emphasize equality of results, rather than equality of opportunity or equality before the law (ideas usually associated with classical liberalism or political libertarianism). In practice, egalitarian policies usually attempt to bring about the equal distribution of wealth, sometimes verging on socialism.

Egoism

[From Latin ego: I, i.e., the self; transliterated from the Greek ἐγώ.]

Ethics: The view that the self is the proper beneficiary of a person's actions, as opposed to the view that other people are the proper beneficiaries (i.e., altruism). Essentially, another word for individualism. The term 'egoism' is used more frequently in philosophy than 'egotism', which in common usage implies an utter disinterest in or disregard for other people.

Emotionalism

[From English emotion: a mental-physical passion, disturbance, or movement; derived from Latin emovere: to move out.]

Ethics: Any ethical theory that is based on feeling as opposed to reason; the term often has connotations of nihilism or irrationalism.

Epistemology: Any theory of knowledge that considers feeling to be a valid means of knowledge (similar to but less intellectualistic than intuitionism).

Emotivism

[From English emotive: pertaining to feeling or passion; derived from Latin emovere: to move out.]

Ethics: A doctrine in 20th-century philosophy that held value-judgments to be nothing more than expressions of emotion (e.g., 'Hitler is evil' really means 'Boo Hitler!'); an extreme form of subjectivism.

Empiricism

[From Greek empeirikos: relating to or derived from experience.]

Epistemology: A theory of knowledge holding that experience is the most reliable source of knowledge. In general, empiricism emphasizes induction over deduction and reality over theory (as, for instance, in the essays of 16th century philosopher Francis Bacon). More specifically, the school of empiricism in the 17th and 18th centuries reacted against the excesses of medieval scholasticism and rationalism by formulating a more systematic grounding for empirical knowledge. The founder of that school was John Locke (1632-1704), whose epistemology tended towards representationalism rather than realism, leading eventually to the skepticism of David Hume (1711-1776). By empiricism is sometimes meant more narrowly a focus on scientific experiment; however, a more appropriate term for that view is scientism or experimentalism.

Environmentalism

[From English environment: the physical and biological conditions of a particular area, often extended to apply to the entire planet; derived from Old French environ: surroundings.]

Ethics: The view that the health of the biosphere or of planet Earth is more important than technological advancement, economic progress, .

Epicureanism

[From the name of the Greek philosopher Epicurus (341-271 BCE).]

Ethics: A school and theory of ethics that advocated enlightened hedonism. Epicurus held that true pleasure consists in the absence of all bodily pains and mental disturbances, a condition he claimed could be easily achieved through moderation, friendship, and the pursuit of wisdom. While Epicureanism was more individualistic than the competing school of Stoicism, its view of happiness was less activist than that of Aristotelianism and can even be compared to some Eastern views like Taoism. Epicurus founded his school in an Athenian garden in the generation after the death of Aristotle and it flourished throughout the Mediterranean for over 700 years.

Essentialism

[From English essential, having real existence or related to the intrinsic nature of a thing; derived from Latin essentia: being.]

Metaphysics: The view that concepts have real existence; another term for Platonic idealism.

Epistemology: The view that all entities have intrinsic properties that can be discerned by reason (sometimes attributed to Aristotelianism but in fact more akin to Platonism and neo-Platonism.

Eternalism

[From Latin aeternus: an age.]

Metaphysics: The view (opposed to creationism) that the universe is eternal.

Ethnocentrism

[From Greek ethnos: a nation or race of people, and from Latin centrum: middle point.]

Ethics: The doctrine that nations or races of people are the primary social reality and that ethical matters are to be gauged by how they affect the interests of a nation or race; opposed to metaphysical and ethical individualism.

Eudaimonism

[From Greek eudaimonia: good fortune, happiness, flourishing.]

Ethics: Any theory that puts personal happiness and the complete life of the individual at the center of ethical concern. Although the term could potentially be used to refer views that value the flourishing of humanity as a whole (such as humanism and anthropocentrism), in practice it is nearly synonymous with individualism and philosophical egoism. Aristotelianism is perhaps the prototypical form of eudaimonism since it provides a well-rounded account of human flourishing and its ethical centrality. By contrast, existentialism rejects happiness as a bourgeois fantasy, and even Stoicism and Epicureanism advocate not individual fulfillment but only the lack of pain or harmful emotions.

Existentialism

[From Latin existentialis: pertaining to existence.]

Ethics: An influential movement in 20th-century ethics holding that values are not universal but instead that each person must create his own values as a result of living life. Its guiding phrase, formulated by, Jean-Paul Sartre (1905-1980), was "existence precedes essence". Although existentialism was a form of individualism, it was also very much a kind of pessimism and opposed to any attempt at ethical naturalism since it held that there is no stable human nature and therefore that there are no common human values. Some existentialists reveled in the unplanned, haphazard character of experience and therefore could be characterized as proponents of irrationalism or even nihilism. Existentialists were also opponents of eudaimonism, since they thought that the quest for happiness is a bourgeois pursuit showing "bad faith".

Experimentalism

[From English experiment: a controlled test undertaken to test a hypothesis or discover some truth.]

Epistemology: A form of empiricism that considers knowledge gained through scientific experiments to be especially reliable (or to be the only reliable form of knowledge).

Expressionism

[From English express: to represent something (especially a thought or feeling) in words or images.]

Aesthetics: A school of modernism holding that the function of art is to provide a vehicle for the subjective experience or emotional expressions of the artist. Expressionist art could be either representational (as in Edvard Munch's painting "The Scream") or abstract (as in the work of painters such as Jackson Pollock and in critical theories such as those of Clement Greenberg).

Fallibilism

[From Latin fallibilis: liable to be deceived or mistaken.]

Epistemology: The view that all human beings are liable to error. Although there is a kinship between fallibilism and skepticism, the term fallibilism usually refers only to the doctrine in some forms of Christianity that human beings cannot know the mind of God.

Falsificationism

[From English falsify: to prove or show to be false based on evidence or testimony.]

Epistemology: The view, first expounded by Karl Popper (1902-1994), that "the criterion of the scientific status of a theory is its falsifiability, or refutability, or testability." According to Popper, "a theory which is not refutable by any conceivable event is non-scientific."

Fascism

[From Italian fasci: groups (of men), in which the Italian Fascist movement began.]

Politics: A form of nationalistic authoritarianism that originated in Italy and spread throughout other parts of Europe (especially Germany and Spain) and the world. Although fascism was ostensibly opposed to communism because it allowed private property (albeit under tight government control), it did not differ in essentials from other forms of collectivism in the 20th century (in fact fascism was a form of national socialism, in contrast to the international socialism of communism).

Fatalism

[From Latin fatalis: destined, inevitable, necessary, doomed.]

Metaphysics: The view that the fortunes of human beings are pre-determined; it differs from determinism in stressing the negative or tragic nature of life (similar to pessimism) and the inability to modify one's fate.

Feminism

[From Latin femina: woman.]

Politics: A movement of twentieth-century politics holding that the rights of women are equal to those of men. Feminism is sometimes extended to assert that women are superior to men in ethics (e.g., more sensitive or altruistic) or even in epistemology (e.g., more wise or insightful).

Fideism

[From Latin fides: faith.]

Epistemology: Any religious doctrine that emphasizes faith over (even to the exclusion of) reason.

Formalism

[From English form: the shape of a thing or the arrangement of its parts.]

Ethics: A theory that emphasizes adherence to formal rules, usually in preference to the benefits or consequences of human action; an example is deontologism.

Aesthetics: A theory that emphasizes the importance of artistic form, often in preference to artistic content; examples include some varieties of classicism and modernism.

Foundationalism

[From English foundation: the groundwork or substructure of a building or, metaphorically, of a theory.]

Method: An approach to philosophical inquiry that places first priority on defining the underlying principles of a discipline; essentially a kind of reductionism within philosophy.

Freudianism

[From the name of the Austrian psychologist Sigmund Freud (1856-1939).]

Psychology: The theories of Sigmund Freud or the tradition of psychological thought and psychoanalytic practice spawned by his theories. The philosophical importance and influence of Freudianism derives from its view of human nature, which emphasizes the importance of unconscious forces in determining the beliefs and actions of human beings.

Functionalism

[From English function: the operation or performance of a thing.]

Epistemology: The view, developed (and then renounced) by Hilary Putnam (1926-), that the mind can be studied in terms of its cognitive operations independently of the brain and body, and that those operations can be adequately modeled by the manipulation of exclusively formal symbols (such as the symbols of symbolic logic or computer programming).

Gnosticism

[From Greek gnosis: knowledge or insight.]

Ethics: An ancient Christian/pagan movement whose metaphysics was a kind of dualism and pessimism but whose ethics was a kind of individualism and optimism since it stressed the potential divinity of each person.

Hedonism

[From Greek hedone: pleasure.]

Ethics: The principle that the fundamental standard of ethical judgment should be pleasure. Although the term has connotations of sensualism and emotionalism, philosophical hedonists (such as those in the tradition of Epicureanism) advocate an enlightened hedonism that is often a kind of naturalism. Although hedonism is usually a species of individualism, utilitarianism advocates "the greatest pleasure for the greatest number" and thus could be construed as a kind of universalized hedonism.

Hegelianism

[From the name of the German philosopher G.W.F. Hegel (1770-1831).]

System: The philsophy of Hegel and the tradition that began with him. In metaphysics, Hegel advocated a kind of historically-minded absolute idealism, in which the universe would realize its spiritual potential through the development of human society. Hegel's absolute idealism is often contrasted with the subjective or transcendental idealism of Kantianism, on whose innovations – in addition to the metaphysical absolutism of Spinoza (1632-1677) – Hegel based much of his philosophy. In political theory, Hegel advocated an organic theory of the state positing that individuals are merely parts of the whole (a form of collectivism often also attributed to Platonism). Hegel was probably the first philosopher to think of history as a dialectical process, which inspired the dialectical materialism of Marxism.

Henotheism

[From Greek henos and theos: one god.]

Religion: Belief in a particular god without denying the existence of other gods. Historically henotheism was a transitional state between polytheism and monotheism.

Historical Determinism

[See historicism and determinism.]

Politics: The doctrine that the course of history is determined by material or spiritual forces that are not open to human volition or change. Examples include the spiritualized historicism of Hegelianism and the dialectical materialism of Marxism.

Historicism

[From English history: the systematic study of the past; derived from Greek historia: an investigation or account of something.]

Politics: The idea that inexorable laws determine all historical events; the term is essentially equivalent to historical determinism, although without the overtones of Marxism.

Holism

[From Greek holos: whole, complete, entire.]

Metaphysics: The idea that all things and events in the universe are inseparably connected. Holism is opposed to dualism but respects particularism and therefore is also generally opposed to monism (interconnection does not imply unity).

Humanism

[From Latin humanus: relating to or characteristic of human beings.]

Ethics: A focus on human concerns as opposed to the interests of the gods (theism) or the technical issues of philosophy (logicism / scholasticism). Examples include Aristotelianism and Epicureanism in ancient Greece, Confucianism and Taoism in China, Renaissance humanism in Europe, and some forms of transcendentalism and pragmatism in America. Although humanism is often closely associated with secularism and individualism, these connections are not necessary; in fact, humanism is sometimes thought of as a 'religion of humanity' that takes altruism and action for the sake of all humanity as its guiding principle (as in the positivism of August Comte).

Hylozoism

[From Greek hule: wood, material, matter, and from Greek zoe: life.]

Metaphysics: The view that all matter is endowed with life (similar to animism, pantheism, or the monadology of Leibniz).

Metaphysics: The view that all life is a property of matter (similar to materialism).

Idealism

[From Greek idea: archetype, pattern, form, type.]

Metaphysics: In the original, Platonic sense, a theory claiming that the primary reality consists of eternal, unchanging, non-physical archetypes, of which the particular entities perceived by the senses are imperfect copies. The most significant forms of idealism after Platonism are the monadology of Leibniz (a kind of panpsychism) and Hegelianism. Although spiritualism is similar to idealism, it usually refers more to religious, supernatural conceptions of reality than to philosophical theories. The opposite of idealism is materialism.

Epistemology: Any theory holding that valid human knowledge is a matter of mentally grasping non-physical archetypes rather than perceiving (or abstracting concepts from) physical entities.

Illusionism

[From Latin illusionem: deceipt.]

Metaphysics: The idea that the external world is merely an illusion; a radical kind of phenomenalism associated with certain forms of pessimism; first posited by Arthur Schopenhauer (1788-1860).

Immaterialism

[From Latin materialis: relating to matter.]

Metaphysics: A radical form of idealism holding that material things exist only as the ideas or perceptions of a mind.

Immoralism

[From Latin immoralis: opposed to accepted customs or morality.]

Ethics: An idea or intellectual stance (similar to nihilism or skepticism) that rejects conventional morality, systematic approaches to ethics, or even ethics as such. Friedrich Nietzsche (1844–1900) is the most prominent thinker who sometimes claimed to be an immoralist.

Incompatibilism

[From Latin in: not, and from Latin compatibilis: sympathetic or mutually tolerant.]

Metaphysics: The view that a full physical description of the brain would be incompatible with the subjective experience of volition; contrast with compatibilism, determinism, and metaphysical libertarianism.

Indeterminism

[From Latin indeterminatus: not fixed or ordained beforehand.]

Metaphysics: Any view (opposed to determinism and similar to accidentalism) holding that at least some events or human actions are not determined by outside causes; the idea of the "atomic swerve" in Epicureanism is one example.

Individualism

[From Latin individuus: indivisible, inseparable.]

Ethics: Any theory holding that the individual, not any sort of collective entity, is the proper beneficiary of action; thus individualism is essentially the same as egoism and is opposed to altruism or ethical collectivism. Most kinds of ethical individualism are forms of eudaimonism, but this is not true of, for example, existentialism or Stoicism.

Epistemology: The idea that only individual minds (not groups) can come to have knowledge.

Metaphysics: The view that only particular, individual things exist; another word for concretism or particularism.

Politics: Respect for individual rights; often synonymous with libertarianism or classical liberalism.

Instrumentalism

[From Latin instrumentum: an implement or tool.]

Epistemology: The view (similar to pragmatism) that concepts are merely useful instruments, properly evaluated not as true or false but as effective or ineffective.

Intellectualism

[From Latin intellectualis: having to do with mind or knowledge.]

Ethics: The view that knowledge is sufficient for excellence and therefore that a person will do what is right or best as a result of understanding what is right or best; sometimes also called Socraticism.

Method: Another term for rationalism, logicism, or scholasticism.

Intentionalism

[From Latin intentionem: mental effort, attention, purpose.]

Metaphysics: The principle, common to many varieties of epistemological realism, that consciousness is always consciousness of a physical entity or some aspect of reality (and thus that "pure consciousness" does not exist, contrary to some forms of idealism).

Interactionism

[From English interact: to work together or exert mutual influence.]

Metaphysics: A form of dualism asserting that mental events can cause physical events and vice-versa.

Interpretivism

[From Latin interpretari: to explain or understand.]

Epistemology: The view that all knowledge is a matter of interpretation; a form of relativism opposed to objectivism. One extreme example of interpretivism is deconstructionism.

Intuitionism

[From Latin intueri: to look upon, consider, contemplate.]

Epistemology: The view (first associated with Platonism) that all knowledge is gained through intuition, immediate insight, or spiritual vision of a transcendent higher reality.

Ethics: The doctrine that ethical theories are best grounded in moral intuitions about what is right or good. Historically, intuitionism has tended to be a kind of deontologism.

Irrationalism

[From Latin irrationalis: contrary to reason.]

Epistemology: A form of subjectivism holding that knowledge and values are relative to each individual person, thereby denouncing objectivity and elevating irrationality. Both emotionalism and nihilism are varieties of irrationalism.

Islam

[From Arabic islam: submission.]

Religion: A unified religious-political doctrine that advocates a strict monotheism, where the only recognized authority regarding the word of the one God was the Arabian prophet and warrior Mohammed (570-632) as laid down in the Koran. In metaphysics and ethics, it is a form of fatalism since it insists upon absolute submission to the arbitrary will of Allah; in ethics and politics, it is a form of authoritarianism since it insists upon absolute submission to the edicts of Mohammed and his successors. The content of Islam is actively and often violently opposed to rationalism, liberalism, capitalism, feminism, atheism, and all competing religions (from animism to Zoroastrianism).

Kantianism

[From the name of the German philosopher Immanuel Kant (1724-1804).]

System: Although Immanuel Kant is known for transcendentalism or idealism in metaphysics and a subtle constructivism in epistemology, his signature idea was deontologism in ethics. In particular, Kant's fundamental contribution to ethical thought was the categorical imperative, according to which the only actions we can legitimately call moral are those that are done purely for the sake of a universal moral law, not from any personal interest (not even an interest in acting ethically!).

Legalism

[From English legal: relating to law.]

Politics: An early Chinese form of authoritarianism, most often associated with the harsh rule of the Ch'in period.

Liberalism

[From Latin liber: free.]

Politics: The classical meaning of liberalism is an emphasis on the freedom and rights of the individual. Although in America the word now refers to a kind of egalitarianism or even democratic socialism, elsewhere it still refers to something like political libertarianism.

Libertarianism

[From Latin liber: free.]

Metaphysics: The doctrine that human beings have the power of volition (opposed to necessitarianism and determinism).

Politics: A doctrine and movement that espouses every individual's liberty to act in complete freedom as long as they respect the rights of others (primarily by not initiating force or fraud). Libertarianism is similar to classical liberalism and sometimes verges on anarchism.

Logical Positivism

[See logicism and positivism.]

Epistemology: A movement of 20th-century epistemology that developed as a reaction against nineteenth-century idealism by combining logicism and empiricism. The logical positivists tended to argue that only carefully-constructed propositions (preferably formulated in terms of symbolic logic) about strictly-limited factual domains could be true or false, and that any less precise proposition or more wide-ranging theory was metaphysical transcendentalism or sentimental emotionalism. In addition to their somewhat hardline epistemological doctrine, the logical positivists tended to ignore the value-branches of philosophy or even espouse emotivism.

Logicism

[From Greek logikos: of thinking or its methods.]

Epistemology: Logicism is essentially a more polite term for scholasticism: an over-emphasis on logical and technical issues in philosophy as well as a denial of humanism.

Manicheism

[From the name of the Greek theologian Manes or Manicheus (3rd century CE).]

Metaphysics: An early, heretical sect of Christianity holding that good and evil are co-eternal and equally powerful; similar in its dualism to gnosticism.

Marxism

[From the name of the German philosopher Karl Marx (1818-1883).]

Politics: A theory of economics and society asserting that social and political change is determined by control over the means of economic production. Marxism inherited its dialectical understanding of history from Hegelianism, but opposed Hegel's idealism with a supposedly-scientific dialectical materialism. Although many Marxists claim that in theory their philosophy is a form of humanism, in practice Marxist political systems such as Leninism and Maoism have proved to be forms of collectivism and therefore quite the opposite of humanism. (To be fair, in reaction to some of his early followers Marx said that he was not a Marxist.)

Materialism

[From Latin materialis: relating to matter.]

Metaphysics: The view that fundamentally only matter exists. Materialism is opposed to idealism and considers any talk of the soul to be a throwback to the bad old days of spiritualism and vitalism. Because materialists generally assert that matter can be known completely in terms of physical laws (see reductionism), they often lend theoretical support to determinism.

Mechanism

[From Latin mechanisma: machine, contrivance.]

Metaphysics: The doctrine, derived from Cartesianism, that living things are in essence machines.

Meliorism

[From Latin melior: better.]

Metaphysics: The idea (similar to optimism) that society can be improved through appropriate human actions, or that the world is continually improving.

Mentalism

[From Latin mentalis: relating to the mind.]

Metaphysics: The view that fundamentally only mind or spirit exists, or that mind or spirit is the fundamental substance in the universe. This view (a kind of metaphysical idealism) is sometimes called immaterialism since it is directly opposed to materialism.

Modernism

[From Latin modernus: that which exists now.]

Aesthetics: A movement of 20th-century art that opposed traditional representationalism and instead emphasized emotional expressionism or artistic formalism (and sometimes both, as in abstract expressionism).

Monism

[From Greek monos: single.]

Metaphysics: The view (opposed to dualism) that reality consists of only one type of substance, historically either mind (see mentalism) or matter (see materialism).

Monotheism

[From Greek monos: single, and from Greek theos: god.]

Metaphysics: The belief that there is only one god, or that the gods of different religions are in fact different manifestations of the one true god. Monotheism is opposed to other forms of theism such as henotheism and polytheism, as well as to pantheism, agnosticism, and atheism.

Mysticism

[From Greek mustikos: relating to the ancient mystery religions or their adherents; later, having to do with any sacred mystery.]

Epistemology: Any belief in the existence and validity of a human cognitive power above reason or perception – usually a kind of intuition or feeling that enables a person to obtain special insights into god, values, or the nature of the universe. The term "mysticism" usually carries religious connotations; similar views in philosophy proper are irrationalism in epistemology and intuitionism in ethics.

Naturalism

[From Latin natura: the character or course of things.]

Metaphysics: The idea that the universe operates according to its own laws, without intervention by any gods (opposed to theism and spiritualism, but compatible with deism).

Ethics: The view that some or all human values (food, water, shelter, safety, psychological closeness, knowledge, etc.) are based on the characteristics of the human organism. For example, existentialism could be considered a humanistic form of individualism, but it differs from many other forms of humanism in denying ethical naturalism.

Aesthetics: The theory that the purpose of art (especially literature) is to present human experience "as is" without evaluation or the projection of ethical ideals (historically, naturalism developed in reaction to romanticism).

Necessitarianism

[From Latin necessitatem: required, needful, necessary.]

Metaphysics: In essence, necessitarianism is determinism applied to human beings: the doctrine (opposed to metaphysical libertarianism) that human beings do not have the power of volition but are determined in their actions by antecedent, external causes.

Neo-Aristotelianism

[See Aristotelianism.]

Ethics: Any updated variety of Aristotelianism, from the Middle Ages to the present; in particular, a strain of moral philosophy in the late 20th century that resuscitated "virtue ethics" and practical wisdom in opposition to the emphasis on moral rules and deontologism found in Kantianism.

Neo-Confucianism

[See Confucianism.]

Ethics: A modified variety of Confucianism that addressed some of the concerns and views introduced into China by Buddhism (similar in some ways to the changes in Aristotelianism and Platonism that resulted from the rise of Christianity).

Neo-Platonism

[See Platonism.]

Metaphysics: The doctrines of Plotinus (205-270 CE) and his followers, or more generally the tradition of such thought stretching from late antiquity into the Middle Ages and early Renaissance. Neo-Platonism put greater emphasis on Plato's dualism and idealism, even to the point of a spiritualism that early Christian theologians like Augustine found congenial despite the basic pantheism of neo-Platonic ideas. The modern understanding of Aristotelianism is heavily influenced by neo-Platonic interpretations.

Nihilism

[From Latin nihil: nothing, non-existence.]

Ethics: Traditionally, a rejection of common morality or religion. For example, Friedrich Nietzsche (1844-1900) is often said to have been a nihilist because of his opposition to Christianity as well as his perspectivism. More recently, some nihilistic currents of 20th-century thought (e.g., some strains of existentialism) bordered on a kind of activist irrationalism by celebrating the meaninglessness of existence and even wanton destruction for its own sake.

Nominalism

[From Latin nomen: name.]

Epistemology: The doctrine (similar to subjectivism) that words are simply conventionally-accepted symbols or names that human beings happen to use for their own convenience, lacking objective meaning or correspondence to reality. The great movements of nominalistic thought occurred among the Sophists of ancient Greece, in the Middle Ages (see also realism and conceptualism), and in the twentieth century among some advocates of logical positivism).

Objectivism

[From Latin objectum: that which is presented to consciousness.]

Metaphysics: The doctrine that reality exists outside of the mind and that entities retain their identity no matter what human beings think or feel about them; another word for realism, in opposition to subjectivism.

Ethics: The view that there are standards of value and conduct based on the reality of human nature; another term for naturalism.

System: The self-described name for the ideas of philosophical novelist Ayn Rand (1905-1982), usually with a capital 'O'.

Occasionalism

[From Latin occasionem: cause or reason.]

Metaphysics: The view (put forward by certain adherents to Cartesianism) that god actively intervenes to move the body when the appropriate volition occurs and to form an idea in the mind when the appropriate sensation impinges on the body.

Operationalism

[From Latin operari: to work, to labor, to complete a task.]

Epistemology: A kind of radical empiricism holding that the meaning of a word is determined by the specific nature of the physical action or task to which it refers, and that different physical actions have different meanings even if referred to by the same word (e.g., assault with a stick and assault with one's fist are two different operations and thus two different concepts).

Optimism

[From Latin optimus: best.]

Metaphysics: Specifically, the belief of Leibniz (1646-1716) that this is "the best of all possible worlds". More generally, the view (opposed to pessimism) that knowledge and happiness are possible to human beings; in this sense, eudaimonism is a form of optimism.

Organicism

[From Greek organikos: pertaining to or structured like an organ, instrument, or tool.]

Metaphysics: The idea that the universe is or is like a living organism. This view is similar to holism, although holism asserts that all parts of reality are interconnected rather than that the earth or the universe is a living thing.

Aesthetics: The idea (which goes back at least as far as Aristotle) that a work of art should be an organic whole, with all its parts or aspects serving one central purpose.

Pacifism

[From Latin pax: peace.]

Politics: The doctrine that the highest political or social value is peace. Another meaning of pacifism – connected with the actions and views of reformers like Henry David Thoreau, Mahatma Gandhi, and Martin Luther King – is the ideal of non-violence in human affairs (akin to the moral aspect of anarchism).

Panpsychism

[From Greek pan: all and Greek psuche: soul.]

Metaphysics: The idea (similar to animism, pantheism, and organicism) that a world soul is present in everything that exists. The monadology of Leibniz (1646-1716) is one form of panpsychism, since it holds that all physical things consist of little bundles of consciousness he called monads.

Pantheism

[From Greek pan: all and Greek theos: god.]

Metaphysics: The belief that God is the universe and the universe is God – or, more generally, that the universe is divine. While this idea often exists in a 'primitive' form (usually called animism), it has also been expanded upon philosophically, for example by Spinoza (1632-1677).

Particularism

[From Latin particularis: relating to a part or an individual.]

Metaphysics: The view that only particular entities exist; another term for metaphysical individualism or concretism.

Perfectionism

[From Latin perfectionem: completed, finished.]

Metaphysics: The view that human beings can achieve perfection in this life; also called perfectibilism.

Ethics: The view that moral perfection is or should be the goal of living.

Personalism

[From Latin persona: a character in a play, the person so represented, an individual having legal rights and status.]

Ethics: The view that the individual person is of supreme value; another term for individualism.

Perspectivism

[From Latin perspectivus: having to do with sight or vision.]

Epistemology: The view (similar to contextualism) that judgments of truth and value depend on an individual's context or viewpoint. The term is usually applied only to the epistemology of Friedrich Nietzsche (1844-1900).

Pessimism

[From Latin pessimus: worst.]

Metaphysics: Specifically, the view of Arthur Schopenhauer (1788-1860) that reality and human nature are essentially malevolent. More generally, the view (opposed to optimism) that knowledge and happiness are ultimately unattainable; degrees of pessimism range from mild (e.g., Stoicism) to severe (e.g., fatalism).

Phenomenalism

[From Greek phenomena: appearance.]

Epistemology: A form of subjectivism or relativism holding that concepts describe only how things appear to human beings and therefore do not result in reliable knowledge of reality.

Physicalism

[From Greek phusis: nature.]

Metaphysics: A form of materialism (stronger than concretism) holding that physical entities are the only real existents and that mental phenomena like soul and consciousness are either illusory or reducible to physical phenomena. Physicalism is often associated with determinism and reductionism.

Platonism

[From the name of the Greek philosopher Plato (427-347 BCE).]

Philosophy: The doctrines of Plato or the tradition of philosophizing that he founded. Usually the term refers to Plato's idealism and dualism, though it sometimes also refers to his collectivism, rationalism, intellectualism, distrust of art, etc.

Pluralism

[From Latin pluralis: more than one.]

Metaphysics: The idea (opposed to monism) that the universe consists of more than one basic kind of substance (thus dualism is a limited form of pluralism).

Politics: The idea that a system of government should allow more than one political party (roughly equivalent to democracy as opposed to totalitarianism).

Polylogism

[From Greek poly: many, and from Greek logos: reason.]

Epistemology: A form of relativism (similar to perspectivism) holding that there are many equally valid theories or beliefs about any given topic.

Polytheism

[From Greek poly: many, and from Greek theos: god.]

Metaphysics: A form of theism holding that there is more than one god; it is compatible with henotheism but incompatible with monotheism, by which it was supplanted in the history of Western religion. Polytheism was the dominant view in ancient Greek and Roman religion, whereas Judaism, Christianity, and Islam are monotheistic.

Positivism

[From French positif: real, actual, practical, experiential.]

Epistemology: Specifically, the view of August Comte (1798-1857) that the pursuit of knowledge should limit itself to observable phenomena and the laws that determine how those phenomena interact, without any investigation of ultimate causes or metaphysics. More generally, the view that knowledge is reliable only if based on what is immediately graspable or scientifically testable (see logical positivism and falsificationism).

Postmodernism

[From Latin post: after, and from English modernism.]

Epistemology: A radical form of relativism (similar to polylogism and opposed to scientism and objectivism) holding that there are no privileged viewpoints and that objective knowledge is effectively unattainable.

Aesthetics: A late 20th-century theory and practice of art that devalued representationalism and formalism in favor of a kind of eclecticism and experimentalism.

Pragmatism

[From Greek pragmatikos: having to do with action, practical affairs, or matters of fact.]

Epistemology: The view, originated by C.S. Peirce (1839-1914) and made famous by William James (1842-1910) and James Dewey (1859-1952), that the truth of a concept is to be evaluated by its practical consequences for human affairs.

Ethics: A form of consequentialism that differs from utilitarianism by emphasizing practical action instead of usefulness to others. While pragmatism is thus a kind of humanism, it rejects naturalism and often tends to be a kind of relativism.

Prescriptivism

[From Latin prescriptionem: a precept or rule.]

Ethics: The view that the function of ethics is to tell people what they should do, not merely to describe what people actually do (thus opposed to descriptivism).

Probabilism

[From Latin probabilis: something provable, credible, believable.]

Epistemology: The idea that certain knowledge is unattainable (similar to fallibilism), but that probable belief provides a firm enough basis for practical living (similar to pragmitism).

Progressivism

[From Latin progressus: stepping forth, going ahead.]

Politics: A political movement that attempts to push society away from established practices (thus in opposition to conservatism).

Psychologism

[From Greek psuchologia: the study of soul or consciousness.]

Metaphysics: The idea that psychology will eventually supersede philosophy by providing scientific answers to the traditional problems of philosophy.

Pythagoreanism

[From the name of the Greek philosopher Pythagoras (6th century BCE).]

Metaphysics: An ancient Greek philosophical movement that emphasized mathematics, numerology, and cosmological harmony. Closely related to Pythagoreanism was the religious sect of Orphism, which held similar views but which was more a form of asceticism.

Rationalism

[From Latin rationalis: having the power of reasoning.]

Epistemology: Specifically, a tradition of philosophy in the 17th and 18th centuries that emphasized deductive reasoning and focused on the "hard" branches of philosophy (e.g., epistemology) instead of the value branches (e.g., ethics, politics, and aesthetics); the most prominent rationalists were Descartes (1596-1650), Leibniz (1646-1716), and Spinoza (1632-1677). More generally, any philosophy that is overly deductive and attempts to mold reality to fit its theories rather than the other way around; in this sense Platonism is a form of rationalism.

Realism

[From Latin realis: relating to things.]

Metaphysics: The notion that concepts or ideas exist in a separate realm of reality (most famous from the Theory of Forms in Platonism); in this sense, metaphysical realism is nearly synonymous with metaphysical idealism and is usually contrasted with nominalism.

Epistemology: The idea that concepts have actual referents in reality and therefore that human beings can and do possess reliable knowledge, both perceptual and conceptual, about reality (essentially a kind of optimism about the possibility of knowledge). In the psychology and philosophy of perception, realism comes in two flavors: direct realism is the principle that human beings perceive the actually existing physical world, whereas indirect realism is another term for representationalism.

Aesthetics: With regard to the visual arts, realism is the portrayal of scenes, objects, and people in ways that are immediately intelligible to the viewer; this is often called representationalism and is usually contrasted with abstractionism. With regard to literature, realism is a focus on the often-gritty reality of life as it is, without the idealization inherent in romanticism; this usage is sometimes also applied in the visual arts.

Reductionism

[From English reduce: to resolve or analyze something into its constituent elements.]

Method: Reduction of complex phenomena into their constituent elements or into simpler or more fundamental phenomena. Both physicalism and behaviorism are examples of reductionism, and reductionism is often closely allied with materialism and determinism. (Sometimes also called reductivism.)

Relationalism

[From Latin relationem: a reference of one thing to another.]

Metaphysics: The doctrine that relations have a real existence; a form of idealism or objectivism.

Epistemology: The doctrine that all knowledge is relative; a less common term for relativism.

Epistemology: The view (similar to coherentism) that theories can be justified through the relationship between ideas.

Relativism

[From English relative: depending on or determined by a relationship between two entities; not independent.]

Epistemology: The view (opposed to objectivism and realism) that truth and value are relative to an observer or group of observers. One example is cultural relativism, which claims that different cultures have different but perfectly legitimate and equally valid standards of truth and value (see polylogism and postmodernism). Relativism is often another word for subjectivism, although the latter term is more personal and does not generally refer to social forms of relativism.

Representationalism

[From English represent: to present clearly before the mind through description or imagination.]

Epistemology: The idea (opposed to realism) that the only things we can know are our representations of the world (e.g., ideas, perceptions, beliefs, etc.), not the world itself. The term is most often used in discussions of perception; the more general term is phenomenalism.

Aesthetics: The principle (opposed by abstractionism) that visual art should represent reality; sometimes also called realism.

Romanticism

[From French romans: a heroic tale written in a vernacular language.]

Aesthetics: A theory and movement of 19th century art emphasizing a free-flowing style, expression of emotion, and concern with values and personal experience in contrast to the emphasis on artistic rules in classicism. In philosophy the term is often equivalent to emotionalism.

Scholasticism

[From Latin schola: school.]

Method: A focus on academic disputes instead of real-world concerns; the term is applied especially to philosophy and theology during the high to late Middle Ages (circa 1100-1500 CE).

Scientism

[From Latin scientia: knowledge, especially organized or experimental knowledge.]

Epistemology: The view (similar to reductionism) that the methods of the natural or physical sciences are universally valid, and therefore should apply to the social sciences and the humanities as well.

Secularism

[From Latin saeculum: the world.]

Metaphysics: The principle (similar to materialism) that gods and purely spiritual entities do not exist.

Ethics: The idea (similar to humanism) that the affairs of this world should be the most important concerns for ethics and human life.

Sensationalism

[From Latin sensationem: relating to the senses of perception.]

Epistemology: A radical form of representationalism positing that all knowledge is constructed from or consists of pure sensations; some adherents even claim that we have knowledge only of sensations.

Sensualism

[From Latin sensualis: relating to the senses of perception.]

Ethics: A form of hedonism that emphasizes the pleasures of the senses or of the body as opposed to the pleasures of the mind (as in rationalism). For example, Epicureanism was opposed to the ancient Cyrenaic philosophers, who claimed that sensual pleasures are superior to intellectual or emotional pleasures.

Situationalism

[From English situation: a specific combination of circumstances.]

Ethics: The view that particular circumstances deserve to be weighted more heavily in ethical decision-making than general or universal principles.

Skepticism

[From Greek skepsis: inquiry, hesitation, doubt.]

Epistemology: Any theory or approach asserting that all claims to knowledge should be doubted, sometimes verging on solipsism or nihilism.

Social Darwinism

[From English social: relating to human interaction or community, and from the name of biologist Charles Darwin.]

Ethics: A movement in the 19th and 20th centuries that purported to apply the biological insights of scientific Darwinism to human affairs by asserting that the principle of "the survival of the fittest" is true in ethics, politics, and social relations. This view was sometimes seen as an accurate description -- or an inexcusable attempt at justification -- of modern capitalism.

Socialism

[From English social: relating to human interation or community.]

Politics: A form of collectivism that emphasizes state ownership of the means of production and justifies subordination of the individual to the community, but often through democratic means and with less of a totalitarian or authoritarian bent than communism.

Socraticism

[From the name of the Greek philosopher Socrates (?470-399 BCE).]

Ethics: Socrates' doctrine of intellectualism.

Method: Socrates' method of asking questions in order to arrive at universal definitions of concepts such as courage and justice (the "Socratic method").

Solipsism

[From Latin solus: alone, and ipse: self.]

Epistemology: A form of subjectivism or relativism claiming that one cannot know if physical reality or other human beings even exist, since one can know only one's own consciousness.

Spiritualism

[From Latin spiritus: the animating principle of humans or of supposed non-physical beings.]

Metaphysics: The belief that there exist purely spiritual entities that do not have bodies or other physical manifestations, or that there exists a spiritual world or realm above and beyond the physical world.

Epistemology: Another term for mysticism.

Ethics: The view that spiritual concerns are more important than this-worldly concerns (a kind of idealism or asceticism that is opposed to secularism).

Statism

[From English state: the governing body of a sovereign nation.]

Politics: A form of collectivism that advocates government power, control, or ownership; socialism, communism, and fascism are more specific forms of statism.

Stoicism

[From Greek stoa: the portico in Athens at which Zeno (the founder of Stoicism) lectured.]

Ethics: A philosophical school, popular in the Roman Empire, that emphasized the ethical independence of the individual by stressing that "virtue is enough for happiness" and therefore that the psychological state of the individual should not be influenced by the presence or absence of worldly values such as friends, wealth, respect, and honor. Further, the Stoics believed that true virtue or excellence lies in not being affected by outside events and in not experiencing passions or emotions (at least negative emotions), but instead in "living according to reason". In its dualism and modified intellectualism, Stoicism was an heir to Socraticism and was a kind of popularized Platonism that opposed the eudaimonism of Aristotelianism and traditional Greek ethics.

Structuralism

[From Latin structura: that which is arranged in a particular fashion.]

Epistemology: The view that language or society is to be studied in terms of structural units or the arrangement of its parts (opposed, for example, to dynamism); in particular, epistemological structuralism influenced various schools of social, political, and literary theory in the 20th century, often overlapping with Marxism and related political movements.

Subjectivism

[From Latin subjectum: the subject or self that is the seat of consciousness.]

Epistemology: Any doctrine (opposed to objectivism and realism) claiming that truth or value is relative to or dependent on the consciousness of the individual, not objective in any way. In general, subjectivism is a personalized form of relativism that in its most radical forms borders on emotionalism, irrationalism, or even solipsism.

Symbolism

[From Greek sumbolon: mark, token, an object that represents another object or an idea.]

Aesthetics: The theory that the central purpose of art or literature is to present striking aesthetic images (often symbols that stand for concepts or ideas).

Syncretism

[From Greek sunkretidzein: to combine two parties or positions in opposition to a third.]

Epistemology: Any attempt to unify seemingly inharmonious theories or systems of philosophy; usually considered to be a more serious intellectual endeavor than mere eclecticism.

Taoism

[From Chinese tao: track, path, way.]

Ethics: An ancient strand of Chinese thought that stressed the inherent untrustworthiness of appearances, the unity of the real world behind the appearances, the necessity of understanding this real unity spontaneously, the cultivation of one's character so that one could become a free spirit, an ideal of non-activity ("we-wei") that is best understood as doing nothing that is contrary to nature or to your own native character, a focus on inner peace and lack of disturbance, and a kind of libertarian political outlook. In general, Taoism was a reaction against the more conservative and action-oriented tradition of Confucianism, and later forms of Taoism borrowed heavily from Buddhism.

Teleologism

[From Greek telos: end or purpose, and from Greek logos: reason, theory.]

Metaphysics: The view that ends or purposes are active, causative forces in the world, especially in the realm of biology (opposed to Darwinism) and sometimes history (see historical determinism).

Theism

[From Greek theos: god.]

Metaphysics: Any belief in the existence of a god or divine powers. While the true opposite of theism is atheism or agnosticism, in Western philosophy theism is sometimes contrasted with deism or with pantheism, in which case it refers either to the active involvement of God in the world or to the separation of God from his creation.

Thomism

[From the name of Christian theologian Thomas Aquinas (?1225-1274).]

System: The doctrines and legacy of Thomas Aquinas, who created a synthesis between Christianity and Aristotelianism that was quite influential in the scholasticism of the later Middle Ages; a particular form of neo-Aristotelianism.

Totalitarianism

[From English totality: the whole or entirety.]

Politics: Advocacy of a society in which government possesses total control over the individual and all mediating institutions such as corporations, associations, and unions; in other words, authoritarianism or political collectivism taken to its logical conclusion.

Transcendentalism

[From Latin transcendentalis: going beyond or above something.]

Metaphysics: Any approach to philosophy holding that there is an aspect of reality higher than the physical world of perception and experience; another term for idealism, often used to refer to Kantianism or even spiritualism.

Ethics: A school of nineteenth century American philosophy initiated by Ralph Waldo Emerson (1803-1882); it advocated a combination of optimism and individualism that emphasized self-reliance and self-fulfillment in harmony with nature.

Universalism

[From Latin universalis: relating to all or to everything.]

Ethics: The view (opposed to individualism) that the proper goal of life is the welfare of all human beings; a specific form of altruism.

Ethics: The view (opposed to situationalism) that principles applying to all situations should be weighted more heavily in ethical decision-making than the particulars of time or place; deontologism is one form of universalism.

Utilitarianism

[From English utility: usefulness.]

Ethics: A form of consequentialism, initiated by Jeremy Bentham (1748-1832) and peaking with John Stuart Mill

(1806-1873), that advocated the principle of "the greatest good for the greatest number" in ethics and society. Utilitarianism was usually a form of altruism, although Mill advocated a kind of individualism since he thought that the best way for humanity to make progress was through the achievements of individuals. Utilitarianism has never made a deep impression in American philosophy, where consequentialism has generally taken the form of pragmatism.

Utopianism

[Coined by Sir Thomas More (1478-1535) from Greek ou: not, and from Greek topos: place (literally, "no place").]

Politics: Any view of societal or political relations that advocates the creation of a perfect society; see also perfectionism.

Verificationism

[From English verify: to prove or show to be true based on evidence or testimony.]

Epistemology: The view (similar to operationalism) that the truth or meaning of a statement consists in the methods by which it is verified; see also falsificationism.

Vitalism

[From Latin vitalis: relating to life or living things.]

Metaphysics: The belief (opposed to materialism and determinism) that human beings are not merely physical but contain a spiritual component or vital essence. In practice, vitalism involves a dualism of matter and life. Usually used in reference to certain views popular during the late nineteenth century in reaction against the rise of Darwinism.

Voluntarism

[From Latin voluntarius: relating to the will.]

Metaphysics: Specifically, the doctrine of Arthur Schopenhauer (1788-1860) that the fundamental power in the universe is will. More generally, another term for libertarianism with regard to volition.

Zoroastrianism

[From the name of the Persian thinker Zoroaster (6th or 7th century BCE).]

Metaphysics: A religion of ancient Persia that emphasized the neverending struggle between forces of good and forces of evil (a view which influenced both gnosticism and Manicheism).

4777118R00045

Printed in Great Britain
by Amazon.co.uk, Ltd.,
Marston Gate.